Global Mixed Gender Basketball (GMGB) is a co-ed basketball league that promotes equal play for equal pay. GMGB is the first league to put female and male pro-athletes on the court to compete simultaneously.

Many people didn't see the vision. However, that vison was made clear on September 23rd at Cox Pavilion in Las Vegas. The New Orleans Gators played the Atlanta Heirs with the Gators as the home team.

GMGB has created an environment were high level athletes both men and women professionals can play each other.

The two teams competed in front of a star-studded audience, the Cox was packed with excited fans and high-level basketball and a piece of sports history was made. GMGB is built on equality for the new millennial pro-basketball audience. The teams were stacked with big names in the pro-basketball genre: Carlos Boozer, Lisa Leslie, Angel McCoughtry, Caron Butler, the Gonzalez Twins, Cappie Pondexter, Stromile Swift, Tyrus Thomas, Brittney Griner and Metta World Piece, just to name a few.

The exhibition game ended with basketball fans and critics amazed and impressed as GMGB League paraphernalia sold out. Metta World Peace said, "Tonight was ground breaking, a real game changer. I can't wait until basketball fans all over the world can experience this up close and personal or through television. These women really can play. And Master P knows firsthand basketball and entertainment."

For more information please visit www.globalmixedgenderbasketball.com.

GMGB

GLOBAL MIXED GENDER BASKETBALL

WE MADE HISTORY

WE CAME TOGETHER

NEW ORLEANS
GATORS

WE WORK HARD

MEN AND WOMEN ON ONE COURT

WE ENTERTAIN

WE NEVER GIVE UP

WE BOUT THE COMMUNITY

WE LOVE OUR FANS

ATLANTA HEIRS
· HEIRS ·   1   NEW ORLEANS GATORS
· GATORS   3   1ST   9:38   2T

WE GO HARD

NEW ORLEANS
GATO

WE ABOUT
BUSINESS

GMGB

WE BELIEVE

ATLANTA HEIRS
HEIRS •   22   NEW ORLEANS GATORS
                              GATORS   16   1ST   3:32   21

GMGB

WE REPRESENT

| ATLANTA HEIRS
HEIRS | 24 | NEW ORLEANS GATORS
GATORS | 18 | 1ST | 2:39 | 17 |

WE INSPIRE

ATLANTA HEIRS
2 HEIRS ▸   19   NEW ORLEANS GATORS
                                1 GATORS   14   1ST   4:55   24

GMGB

WE ARE ABOUT LOVE

WE ARE ABOUT PEACE

WE ARE ABOUT CHANGE

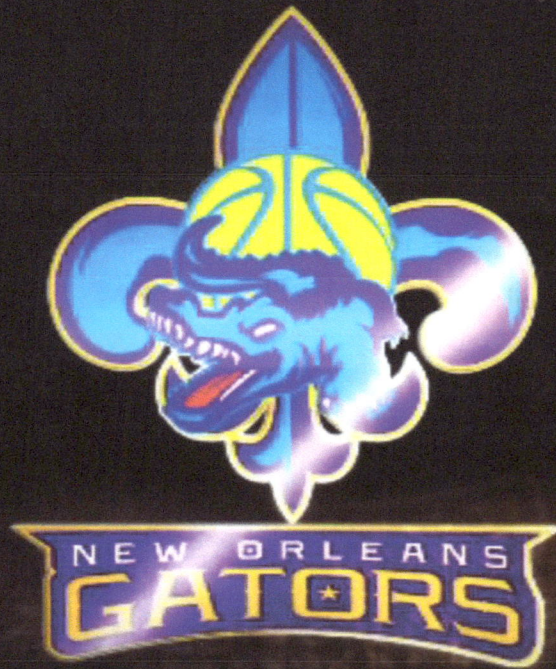

NEW ORLEANS
GATORS

EQUALITY

WE STICK TOGETHER

WE THINK BIG

WE ABOUT THE NEXT GENERATION

WE CHANGING THE GAME!

www.ingramcontent.com/pod-product-compliance
Lightning Source LLC
Chambersburg PA
CBHW040711150426

42811CB00061B/1827